Praise for *Birthday Gifts: Honoring People and Places We Love*

Birthday Gifts takes us on a journey through time and space. Each one of these stories shows us that it is not the cake, decorations, or the gifts that make the birthdays special, it is the people, places, love, and kindness. Michelle M. Jacob reminds us to "savor the present moment, find delight in the gifts all around us, and celebrate what brings us joy."

—Marta Clifford (Chinook, Cree, Grand Ronde), Tribal Elder

Birthday Gifts is tender, gentle, and filled with powerful love. Each individual story is special and important but it's the collection that does much more with its impact.

—Meggin McIntosh, The PhD of Productivity

What a gift it is to learn, laugh, and remember with the beautiful lessons of *Birthday Gifts*. Michelle M. Jacob generously shares birthday stories—personal and always grounded in Yakama lifeways—that offer needed teachings and wisdom for young and elder readers alike!

—Django Paris, Director, Banks Center for Educational Justice, University of Washington

Birthday Gifts is packed with beautiful wisdom and is engagingly written from start to finish.

—Amy Lonetree (Ho-Chunk), Author of *Decolonizing Museums*

Also by Michelle M. Jacob

Yakama Rising: Indigenous Cultural Revitalization, Activism, and Healing

Indian Pilgrims: Indigenous Journeys of Activism and Healing with Saint Kateri Tekakwitha

On Indian Ground: A Return to Indigenous Knowledge: Generating Hope, Leadership, and Sovereignty through Education in the Northwest (co-edited with Stephany RunningHawk Johnson)

The Auntie Way: Stories Celebrating Kindness, Fierceness, and Creativity

Huckleberries & Coyotes: Lessons from Our More than Human Relations

Fox Doesn't Wear a Watch: Lessons from Mother Nature's Classroom

Anakú Iwachá: Yakama Legends and Stories, 2nd Edition (co-edited with Virginia R. Beavert and Joana W. Jansen)

Birthday Gifts

Honoring People and Places We Love

Written by
Michelle M. Jacob

Illustrated by
Crystal L. Buck

ANAHUY MENTORING, LLC
EXCELLENCE IN INDIGENOUS METHODS

Author royalties are donated to the Sapsik'ʷałá Program at the University of Oregon to support the next generation of Indigenous teachers. By purchasing this book, you are supporting Indigenous self-determination in education. Kw'ałanúushamash! (I am grateful to you!)

ISBN (paperback): 978-1-7346151-6-6
ISBN (e-book): 978-1-7346151-7-3

Cover design by Christopher J. Andersen
Cover illustration by Crystal L. Buck

Library of Congress Control Number:
2022914825

Whitefish, MT
Indigenous homelands of Salish, Kootenai, and Pend d'Oreille peoples, taken in the Hellgate Treaty of 1855

https://anahuymentoring.com
https://auntieway.com

This book is dedicated to educators—past, present, and future—who bring kindness, fierceness, and creativity into our lives. Your work is such a blessing to us!

Contents

Introduction: Invitation to Black Bear's Birthday Party

Welcome! I'm so glad you're here. Thank you for being a guest to Black Bear's birthday party.

The title of this chapter comes from my beloved Rez Dog, Anahúy, a common dog name on my Yakama Reservation, and the name means Black Bear.

Black Bears are special beings in our Yakama culture. We have traditional stories that remind us of the ways Black Bear is a helpful, thoughtful being. Our beautiful stories invite us to listen and learn through observation and deep reflection. It is education designed to connect generations, teach the importance of place, and remind humans of our sacred, honorable, and humble responsibility to care for one another and all beings.

Traditionally, our Yakama education doesn't have formal grades that students progress through, or are held back from, every academic year. We don't traditionally have paper diplomas and official transcripts or letter grades that rate our learning as A to F, which are then calculated into a grade point average. We also don't traditionally define education as schooling systems in which the people in power-making decisions about curriculum, pedagogy, and teacher certification may not ever step foot onto our Indigenous homelands; they may not ever witness firsthand the strength and beauty of our relationships and cultures.

Rather, our people understand education as a process that must always be in respectful relationship with place, and like Niní (Aspen Tree), we soak in the teachings around us and are grateful for our strong root systems and webs of kin. We grow and change in the process—wisdom from our Elders continually strengthening our roots. As we learn more teachings, our trunks become stronger, ready to support our beautiful branches and leaves of life.

Our culture honors the importance of strong individuals—it is up to every one of us how each of our branches and each of our leaves grow in this world. What remarkable freedom and responsibility we entrust ourselves and one another with. Our teachings also share the importance of the power of the collective. Don't you see? In our beautiful grove we are all connected, like Niní. Therefore, it is important for me to care that your roots are healthy and vital. My writing this book is one expression of care, with the hopes that the loving messages in this book will be a source of comfort, hope, and learning for all readers. Your health and well-being matter to me. Keeping toxic harm away from you matters to me. We are all connected in this beautiful collective.

These are teachings that have sustained our people Since Time Immemorial. We treasure our stories. We treasure our ways of knowing and being. And we carry our treasured teachings with us in the world today.

When we honor and celebrate one another's birthdays, we are engaging in our people's timeless practice of affirming our strong community and family relationships. We also engage in gift giving to uphold our practices of sharing, reciprocity, and generosity as ways to communicate that another person is important to us.

When a group comes together to celebrate a person's birthday, we are affirming that person is valuable and honored in our community. We can engage our traditional stories, songs, prayers, and foods at birthday celebrations, and we can bring in other traditions as well. For example, Shoshone-Paiute "Auntie Steph" reminds me that birthdays can be focused on celebrating a person's mother, who gave birth on that day.

There are many ways that birthdays can

be celebrated, whether at the longhouse, the skating rink, a pizza restaurant, or a park by the river; in a classroom or a loved one's home; or at any special gathering place.

Throughout the many examples, venues, and ways of celebrating, one key lesson remains: As strong communities, we honor the presence and importance of each person. And one way of doing that is to celebrate birthdays.

In this book, I take the idea of a birthday—the honoring and celebrating of another year of life—and tell stories about beautiful kindnesses I've witnessed. In this way of experiencing the world, each year is precious in our journey of gathering up wisdom, as we mark the number of times while on this precious Mother Earth we've rotated around Aan (Sun). Aging can be a special and graceful process because of our deepening sense of love and care for those around us, and for ourselves.

Stories in this book take place on my Yakama homelands and at special places I've been fortunate to visit. I invite you to relax in one of your favorite places, perhaps among some of your favorite people, and enjoy reading the stories. I also invite you to engage your own wisdom and sweet memories that I hope are prompted by the discussion and journaling questions following each story.

When we are fortunate to take time and space to savor memories of special people and places, we can identify and soak up some of life's most precious teachings—this is true nourishment! Each reader has a unique perspective and set of experiences from which to draw—how lovely to know that perhaps a million or more different memories will be prompted by all our memories and engagement with our deeper wisdom that we've gathered throughout our lives.

Sometimes birthdays are thought of in terms of sweet treats, decorations, and maybe a lavishly wrapped present. However, in this book, although I refer to the material aspects of birthday celebrations, over and over I return to an important lesson that instructs us otherwise. Throughout this book, I share how memories of special people, special places, and the kindnesses we extend to one another are in fact our most treasured gifts.

Thank you for being here. It is one of my greatest hopes that this book is nourishing for your own roots, trunk, branches, and leaves. I am honored to be part of your beautiful grove, as we age together, gracefully.

Your health, well-being, and presence are important. I wish you a day, year, and lifetime of good nourishment.

Let's celebrate!

Elder Birthdays

I think all birthday parties are fun, in some way. But some more than others. For example, I love birthday parties celebrating Elders.

I enjoy being around Elders. This may be due to the routine begun with my auntie and my mom when I was younger. One of them would load me in the car, and we'd go all around the reservation visiting elderly friends and relatives.

"Bring something to show them," sometimes I'd be instructed before we got into the car.

So I'd grab my small collection of rocks or a sticker album in which I'd placed some extra special stickers, perhaps a shiny foil sticker of a teddy bear or a fuzzy heart or flower, purchased from those rolls on pretty display at the Hallmark store in Yakima.

We'd get to the Elder's house, and we were greeted at the door. Sometimes right away, and sometimes we'd have to wait "for my creaky old bones to get moving," they might say, as they reached out to open the screen door for us, thin, crepe-like skin on their hands and arms and a warm smile on their wrinkly face. I could tell by the way Auntie and Mom conducted themselves that these Elders we visited were the personification of wisdom. Do you know the feeling? When someone you trust feels great respect toward another person or being? The honor and gratitude they feel is palpable in some way. It's a nice feeling, a good teaching.

Next we'd have tea or water, or if I was lucky something glamorous like lemonade or Sunny Delight.

Maybe some of those long rectangle wafer cookies would be set on a plate. Now I'm not sure about these cookies. They kind of remind me of colorful Styrofoam. But they're easy to eat—they almost dissolve in your mouth, and they do taste good, those airy layers of cookie and some kind of crème-like filling. They are light and sweet. My grandma used to purchase the ones that came in what some cookie packages refer to as Neapolitan colors—that bright pink along with sandy, muddy-colored brown and the creamy light tan that we think of as vanilla colored.

Uncle Chris sometimes purchases the chocolate version of those cookies. Maybe it's some kind of wisdom superfood, as he's one of the wisest guys I know.

Back to visiting with Elders—Mom or Auntie would chat with them about how all the family is doing. We'd hear the updates on the Elders' health problems and all the latest news from our common acquaintances. Perhaps discussion about the weather would take place, or comments on the progress of the Elder's favorite tree or plant or hedge in their garden, or one they could see in the yard from a nearby window, if their hands-on gardening days were over.

And then perhaps I'd be invited to go sit close to the Elder and show what I'd brought. "I brought my rocks," I might say.

"Is that right? Let me see, Honey. Oh, that's a nice one. Which one's your favorite?"

"This one." I'd pick up the small, smooth round rock with a pretty purply, lavender color. I would gently touch the smooth surface of the favored rock before handing it to the Elder.

"Oh, how beautiful!" They'd admire the rock closely, working hard against their failing eyesight. "Oh, yes, I see! You know, this is a special rock. It reminds me of the same color I saw when I was young and went up to Mt. Rainier and the lupine were in full bloom. Oh! I'll never forget that sight. Meadows full of them! Purple waves of these gorgeous flowers all around me. Can you imagine? Just beautiful! You see something like that and you never ever have to question if Creator loves you. Do you know that? Creator loves you. And gives you this pretty rock and meadows full of lupine so you remember."

A gentle smile is on the Elder's face. The love and care in their story paint a perfect picture for me. Elders have a way of telling you the profound teachings they've learned in their long lives. They have a way of sharing big truths and important lessons in simple and succinct ways. I'm not sure how they do this with such seeming ease. Perhaps it's because of a special secret magic wisdom of Elders that they somehow pick up over their many years and decades.

We sit in silence for several moments, and I observe the Elder, their kindly face that's weathered many storms of life. Some might say Elders are frail and weak, but if you look closely, you can see the ironclad strength of their spirit. It shines unmistakably in their eyes. Even the clouds of cataracts cannot mask it.

"Okay," I say, letting the Elder know I've received their important teachings, the gifts they've offered me.

The Elder smiles a bit wider, skin around their eyes crinkly with joy.

"Good," the Elder affirms and hands me back the rock.

My Auntie or Mom, at this point, would likely set their cup or mug down with enough noise to communicate without vocalizing, "It's time for us to go."

We help with the dishes and put things away, see if garbage needs to be taken out, and always check if there is anything urgent from town that they need. We say our "See you later" greetings and head back out to the car.

If no errands need to be run, we ride home, and I hold the rock in my small hands, hoping that we'll get to visit the lupine meadows the Elder described. I can picture the glaciers of Ta<u>x</u>úma as a beautiful background to the pretty flowers. Isn't it wonderful how Elders' stories can help us dream and imagine inspiring futures for ourselves?

Several decades later I find myself sitting next to another Elder. It's a large party in a room full of people singing the "Happy Birthday" song with great enthusiasm, first in English and then in Ichishkíin sɨ́nwit, our Indigenous language. "Happy birthday to you!! Happy birthday to you!! Kw'ałáni mash wa páwyakyut łkw'i!! Kw'ałáni mash wa páwyakyut łkw'i!!"

When the singing finally ends, the Elder blows out the candles and everyone cheers. The huge cake is sliced and shared; Elders are served first, to honor their status in our community. I see at this birthday gathering there are also pies, like my dad remembers from his childhood birthday celebrations, with the kind of light, flaky crust he described that was skillfully made in my grandmother's kitchen, without any measuring cups or spoons—she just knew the right amount of ingredients to use. Of course, the fruit filling is just the right consistency and sweetness. Mmmmm…

I turn my attention away from the sweet treats and notice the Elder is gazing around the room; surely they see we are surrounded by love and care. Soon perhaps there will be speeches, gift giving, and maybe we'll even pose for some group photos. In my community, as well as in many others, birthday celebrations are a wonderful way to gather up loved ones and reaffirm what matters to us: honoring and respecting one another, through the ups and downs of life, and all the challenges our communities face. We know we are always stronger together.

I take another bite of the delicious cake, and then I look into the Elder's eyes and see that unmistakable magical combination of ironclad strength and the wisdom of a long life.

What a gift.

Discussion/Journaling Questions for "Elder Birthdays"

1. Think of a time when you were in the presence of someone wise and respected. How did you feel? In your opinion, how do wise and respected people conduct themselves?

2. Think of the traits that wise and kind Elders have. In what circumstances do you demonstrate some of these same traits?

Beautiful Cake

Growing up, we never bought cakes from the grocery store. I've always admired the pretty decorations, fancy piped frosting, sprinkles, or pearl-shaped sugar candies. Sometimes they had big colorful frosting flowers on top and slivered almonds all around the edges. And, of course, big, beautiful cursive writing that read, "Happy Birthday!" I could stand there in the bakery department at the Toppenish Safeway and stare at the cakes like an art connoisseur at the Louvre. If I stood there too long, and Mom had already completed her shopping for the week, she would not have the patience to come look for me. Instead, she'd have me paged over the grocery store loudspeaker; "Michelle, your mother is waiting for you at the front of the store," the grocery store manager's voice would boom over the speaker.

Oh! The embarrassment of hearing one's name blasted out on the speakers for all the shoppers to hear. Mom was really practical like that. I can see how, in a way, she was cutting edge. Nowadays a text message can be sent. "I'm checking out." Or "Ready." And the rendezvous could happen without a public announcement. Sigh. But not in my youth; we had never heard of a cellular phone, nor could we imagine a computer that could fit in your pocket.

Rushing to the front of the store, I dreaded the embarrassing message would repeat over the loudspeaker if I didn't get there in time. I knew better than to complain, though. Mom didn't like me to wander off, and if I did so, I knew I was gambling. Like a tough blackjack dealer at the casino, Mom would have no trouble sweeping my chips off the table if I'd made a bad decision and lost track of time admiring the cakes. Busted!

As I told you, we never bought those cakes when I was growing up. Mom made every single birthday cake every year for our large family. On my birthday we had at least two cakes each year, as I was born on my brother's birthday, and we celebrated the day with food, family, cake, and gifts enough to saturate that day with birthday goodness. We got to pick which flavor of cake and frosting. Usually, the cake was made from a boxed mix. Frosting was always homemade. Mom has strong feelings that the frosting in a can doesn't taste good, I think. And as for the bakery cakes, I think they were perceived as either too expensive or not tasting good—or maybe both. I'm not quite sure, but I knew they were off limits, the forbidden dessert.

So imagine my surprise when my grandfather turned 80 years old and an order for a large custom cake was placed! "Aunt" Dorothy, a family friend who baked cakes as a side business, made it for our special occasion. I still remember that massive box it came in and the hope and excitement and anticipation of seeing the lid first opened. Wow! That pretty piped frosting. It had such a beautiful design—a train! My grandpa loved trains and spent most of his life living right next to the railroad tracks. And such a tall cake. It had layers!

As you know by now, I love cakes. And my grandpa and I had a special closeness. Oh the hours and hours we'd spend listening to Mariners games on the radio or watching *The Price Is Right* or *Wheel of Fortune* on television. So perhaps for these reasons, I was given the extra special honor of carrying Grandpa's cake out to the picnic table on the patio, where he was sitting and visiting with friends and relatives—one of the biggest gatherings I've ever seen at my parents' house.

Well, let me tell you something about my parents' house. To go from the kitchen out to the patio one must walk down two steps. Now please also remember I was a bit of a shy child. So the candles were lit. Fancy candles bought at the store shaped into an "8" and a "0." We'd never gotten those extravagant candles before. So there I was, a shy girl with skinny arms carrying a candlelit cake—the biggest, heaviest cake I've encountered in my life. Someone opened the door to the patio for me. Everyone looked and ooooohs! and aaaaahs! I believe they started singing the "Happy Birthday" song to my beloved grandpa.

And then, somehow, maybe you've guessed this, I tripped on those two steps.

You know how sometimes everything is going in a dizzying, fast-forward pace, but also somehow time seems to almost stand still? This was one of those moments, with thoughts of, Oh no! I'm tripping! Oh no! This cake is so heavy! Oh no! What's happening?

Splat!!!

The heavy cake was destroyed.

There was a mix of "Oh no!" "Holy crap!" "Honey, are you ok?" And, of course, gut-busting laughter at my unintentional slapstick performance.

One of my elderly uncles told me, "If I would've known you were going to do that, I would've given you five bucks to throw it at my sister!" And then his face crinkled in that way that Elders' faces do when they smile and laugh from deep within, a laugh so rich and joyful that one cannot help but join in and also give your knee a slap while doing so.

"Oh, shut up!" one of my elderly aunts snapped at Uncle, overhearing his comment to throw the cake at her. It's not often one can witness people in their 80s argue with their siblings. My aunts scooped up the cake from the ground and served it on little plates, with forks and special napkins bought for the occasion. "Here, this part didn't touch the ground. And besides, the patio was just swept," they encouraged attendees. My aunties' voices, rough from decades of cigarette smoke, had enough authority in their tone to make sure no one challenged whether the cake was edible. My Depression-era grandpa and his siblings all chimed in, "Waste not, want not," as they munched on the messy, squished cake.

Well, the great cake fiasco was several decades ago, of course, and we all survived and had a good laugh. Grandpa was diabetic so maybe it was better he didn't have a bunch of cake leftovers tempting him and sending his blood sugar numbers sky-high.

Even today, I still enjoy looking at those beautiful cakes in bakery displays. When I see that fancy piped frosting, I always think of my grandpa and the cake never properly served. I can laugh now, remembering that terrible sight of the beautiful cake "splat" on the patio. Standing in the bakery, smiling and looking at the pretty cakes, I don't know if they taste good.

But I do know they always help me remember the precious memories of life and loved ones. And that is the sweetest treat of all.

Discussion/Journaling Questions for "Beautiful Cake"

1. Think of a time when you felt shame or disappointment over a mistake. Who helped you feel better? Or how might you help someone having a difficult moment?

2. If you could design any cake for a loved one, what would you include in your design? Why? For fun, do a quick sketch of your idea or tell someone about it.

If you're on Twitter, you can share your design idea by tagging @AnahuyMentoring

A Royal Birthday

In this story, I'm going to describe royalty and the things they do on special occasions: with whom they spend their time, what they wear, and what they do. You know, how the royal family in England receives so much attention. Millions of people watch television and purchase magazines and tabloids to find out what they're doing; there's a seemingly endless appetite to know with whom they spend their time, and, of course, there is great excitement to find out what they are wearing.

Well, this story shares some similarities, but it is also quite different. The whole notion of empire and the project of taking wealth from other peoples' lands or the stealing of lands in settler colonialism—the very foundation of royalty and the wealth of nation-states to-day—these are all greedy and immoral from an Indigenous perspective. Yet we do see a tradition in Indigenous communities of honoring royalty.

We have Treaty Days royalty, Pow Wow royalty, and even royalty at rodeos. My nephews are sometimes crowned Homecoming Prince at the public school on our reservation. Yet these versions of royalty on and around our Indigenous homeland are different. They indicate status bestowed on young people who are considered to be role models among their peers. Often royalty status is something that is earned based on the work a young person does to learn. Perhaps they have dedicated time to learn their Indigenous cultural teachings and then shared those teachings with a broader audience. In doing so they are stepping forward to show their leadership potential, skills, and ability—to represent themselves, sure, but more importantly to represent our people in a respectful way that helps to create a proud future for us all. In this way, we are taking the idea of royalty and making it our own, which I think is a fabulous way to exercise self-determination.

These examples I am discussing are formal ways that the notion of royalty are reimagined and upheld in our community. We play with the idea of royalty in informal ways as well. Such is the spirit of the story that I'll now share with you.

Sometimes birthdays are celebrated at special places.

I have not been to the dining establishment Burger King for a long time. However, I remember in my childhood when I was there and, at least in Yakima, on the counter by the cash registers they had those lovely looking paper crowns. They came flat and you had to bend them into a circle and fasten the tab into the proper slit to fit your head size. Then, perhaps with some flair, don the crown. Ah! The crown was golden colored with big rubies and sapphires and emeralds (I believe that is what the red, blue, and green vibrant ink was indicating). I adored it! It was the perfect thing to wear so you could sit regally in the fast-food lobby while awaiting one's birthday breakfast; a Bacon, Egg, and Cheese Croissan'wich accompanied by a small orange juice. Make sure to wipe your hands on a napkin before removing your crown—you don't want to get it greasy.

I remember a birthday like this. My parents took our whole family out to a special breakfast after we went to church early on Sunday. It was so fun! I remember thinking to myself, *We should do this every day!* not understanding how expensive restaurants are for large families. It was early in the morning, and we had the lobby almost to ourselves, fitting for royalty on a special occasion. I remember my brothers blowing the paper sleeves off their straws, aiming for each other, my mom hustling up games of shooting sugar packets across the small tables, trying to get closest to the edge without dropping off the table—and a festive competitiveness arising among anyone who engaged the sugar packet arena. Small bets were placed; my dad and I watched with amusement, taking turns heckling and encouraging depending on the ups and downs of the game. We almost always cheer for the underdog.

Decades later, as I peer back in time, I smile with joy and humor filling my spirit. The rich food, boisterous company, gambling, and festivities—I couldn't ask for a better birthday celebration or a finer royal court.

Discussion/Journaling Questions for "A Royal Birthday"

1. Have you played with the idea of being royalty? If so, what did you imagine? If you could choose, who would be in your royal court?

2. Where is a special place of celebration from your younger years? How do you see that place today—do you have a different perspective of it? Would you choose to celebrate in the same place today, or would you choose a different place to celebrate a special occasion?

Mr. Teddy

Have you ever traveled to visit some of your favorite people on your birthday?

I have.

One time, when I was about six years old, we traveled all the way to California to visit my auntie. She was the kind of person who had small and big ways of showing you how she felt, including the way she would tilt her head just slightly and gently smile—the message unmistakable to a child; I love you. I'm so glad you're here, without having to say a word. In that way, Auntie was so simple. She was also kind, gentle, and fiercely stubborn—a quality that served her well when she pursued independence by moving off our reservation for economic opportunities—as a Yakama "Rosie the Riveter" in the World War II factories in Seattle and later in Southern California where she sewed uniforms for the employees at Knott's Berry Farm and did a variety of other contract work as a seamstress.

Although she was mostly a quiet and humble person, Auntie could also be quite formal and extravagant. For example, she would have no problem spending her hard-earned money as a seamstress on the most expensive birthday card she could find at the Hallmark store. I remember one year she bought two of those huge fancy cards for my birthday, with their fine thick cardstock embossed with richly colorful foil. I can see the pretty envelopes with my name scrawled across the front in Auntie's gorgeous, old-fashioned cursive writing. The elaborate cards always had a "Happy birthday to my special niece" message, compliments of the greeting card writers, printed prettily on the fancy cards. And inside was more of Auntie's big, loopy, perfect cursive writing, always in black ink.

When we visited Auntie for my birthday, it was actually a triple party, with celebrations for my brother, uncle, and me. Auntie made sure to cook the biggest feast you had ever seen—I don't know how she did it in her tiny little kitchen, but she and my uncle prepared prime rib, turkey, and ham! And, of course, a huge cake, along with several pies. This over-the-top party made us feel special, and now that I'm older, I can see the practical wisdom in cooking a lot of food for a party when a large family arrives to stay in your home. Guests can help themselves to delicious leftovers throughout their stay.

So after everyone eats until they're stuffed and are "full as a tick," as Auntie would say, we would then think about cards and gifts, which would be opened after dishes were washed and put away. This was my favorite part of the party. I can remember one birthday celebration when, after the cards were opened and read, it was time to open my gifts.

Auntie always poured her love, care, and hope into the clothes she sewed, knitted, and crocheted for me. Everyone would admire her new creations as I held them up after unwrapping them. And then, one birthday, Auntie went to get something under her sewing table. It was a huge box. Like all of Auntie's gifts, it looked professionally wrapped, no lumps or tears or crooked paper to be found—only smooth, straight paper crisply folded, always with a fancy matching bow.

Petite Auntie wrestled the large box from its hiding place and presented me with it. I removed the bow carefully, setting it on a nearby table so it could be reused, as Mom had taught me to do with the less fancy bows that come in a big bag from Bi-Mart. Then, I carefully lifted the paper that had been taped, not tearing it, so it could be reused. My slow and careful efforts were boring my large family, who wanted to move on to cake and pies.

"Just tear it!"

"Rip it! We're not going to reuse it anyway!"

Bossy encouragement came from the audience crowded around the table in Auntie's small dining area.

I complied.

Rip!

Tear!

A huge cardboard box was next. I removed the tape that held the flaps shut. Peeped inside.

Gasp! A huge teddy bear! I struggled to lift him out.

"Oh my goodness!"

"Wow!" admiration came from the audience.

"That's a huge bear! It's almost bigger than you!"

I smiled the biggest smile my face could hold. I hugged the bear, who actually was as tall as me.

"I love him! Mr. Teddy is his name," I introduced the bear to my family.

"Great! Let's have cake," my audience concluded, and the party moved along.

Auntie sat on the couch with me, and I told

her how much I enjoyed my gifts and that I'm sure Mr. Teddy will enjoy living with us and meeting all my other bears.

Now, with the fancy festivities of cards and gifts over, I see the biggest gift of all. That very slight tilt of the head, the gentle smile, the unmistakable love in her eyes shining down on me. I know she loves me, and she's glad I'm here.

Discussion/Journaling Questions for "Mr. Teddy"

1. Think of someone who lets you know they care about you without saying a word. How do they do so? How do you show your care for a loved one?

2. Take a moment to savor a memory of someone special to you. How has this special person made an impact in your life? If, in the future, someone was savoring a memory of you, what would you like them to remember?

Good Ride to the Airport

Some of the highlights of my childhood include the few times I got to go on an airplane to visit my auntie in California. Sometimes I got to go on this fabulous journey on or around my birthday, which happens to be in winter, a time when the family farm is a bit quieter; sure, there is work to do, but when that work happens is a little flexible, unlike many other times of the year when the pace and demands of work barely let up.

To prepare for the airplane trip, my parents, God Bless Them, got each of us a suitcase and put little stickers on them with our initials. Naturally, mine said "MMJ." We were each allowed to put our necessities into our case. Remember to have room for souvenirs and gifts to bring back to family members who'd eagerly await our return and stories from our journey. And, of course, if we were traveling around my birthday, I knew that I needed to leave some room for gifts that my Auntie would give me. She spoiled me, almost to a fault—mine of course, not hers.

Once all the suitcases were packed, we'd all load into the station wagon and drive across our beautiful Yakima Valley, named after our people, and then over the big ridges to the north and up to I-90, that big road carved into the landscape of our people's traditional homelands. We'd drive through the mountains and finally get to the hustle and bustle of the greater Seattle area, Coast Salish homelands. Take 405 South and into the neighborhood of South Center shopping mall, a magical place in and of itself, with its bright lights and big fancy stores. But we had no time for such distractions. We had to catch a flight to my Auntie's! But first we go to my other Auntie's house.

We'd pull into the driveway at her Tukwila home. As always, she and Uncle were peering out the window awaiting our arrival. They'd smile and wave, so joyful! It was like our showing up in their driveway was the equivalent of Christmas or the final wish from a genie who came out of a bottle—something huge like that—that is how special we were made to feel whenever we arrived at their house. They'd hurry down the stairs, throw open their turquoise-painted wooden front door, and rush out to greet us, hands held in the air, joyous laughter coming out of their mouths, big smiles crinkling their faces.

I loved visiting my Auntie and Uncle in Tukwila. Every single time I arrived at their house the greeting was the same—absolutely overflowing with love and joy—to see me, welcome me, no matter the size or severity of my recent accomplishments…or failures.

Even when they became old and frail and no longer able to hurry down the stairs to the front door, they still watched from the upstairs window. Waving a little less vigorously, sure, but that deep, rich, unconditional love sparkled unmistakably in their eyes. What a gift.

So after the greetings, and potty breaks addressed after the long ride in the car, we'd visit a bit. We were highly encouraged to eat a meal or snack. Auntie and Uncle would forbid guests to leave without some kind of sustenance. And then we'd all pile into their station wagon. Luggage stacked in the back. Kids squished into one another on the bench seat. Uncle would drive us on the back roads to Sea Tac. When the air traffic control towers were in sight, we passed a large cemetery.

"That's where we'll be buried," Auntie and Uncle shared, "so when we're gone, you need to wave at us when you go to Sea Tac. We'll sit up and wave back at you!"

We all chuckled softly at this idea. I could definitely see them doing that. That love and care shining brightly in their spirit eyes as they watch over us during our travels, our lives.

Once at the Departures area, Uncle would dock his big black car next to the curb. Hugs, love, smiles, and good wishes would overflow once again. They sent us off on our journey bundled up in layers of kindness and joy.

In remembering these special times, of the thrilling anticipation of a special trip on my birthday, of the family journeys taken to visit loved ones, I see perhaps the greatest, most enduring birthday gift of all was the way my dear Aunties and Uncles showered me with generous lessons on how to be welcoming and loving. This was a gift so large, no wrapping paper or bow could ever contain it. They modeled how to provide a warm and encouraging presence. They affirmed your presence was the greatest present to them.

As I think back on the lessons I've learned from my beloved Aunties and Uncles, this is one of the shining gems: the willingness and ability to show tremendous love and care in the everyday. Every gesture, every word reaffirming how special you are. Now that's a pretty good ride to the airport.

Discussion/Journaling Questions for "Good Ride to the Airport"

1. In "Good Ride to the Airport," the narrator invites readers to reflect on the love and care shown in a simple task like giving someone a ride where they need to go. How have you given or received extraordinary care in a seemingly mundane task? How might you show your love and care in an everyday task in the future?

2. The narrator describes "a gift so large, no wrapping paper or bow could ever contain it." When have you given or received a gift like this? If you could give any gift to a loved one, what would it be?

Birthday
PRIZE BOX

Prize Box

I remember when I was a college student far away from home in California, on Luiseño/Payómkawichum Indigenous homeland, how much fun birthdays could be. Now, it didn't really matter whose. Any birthday was fun—Academic Auntie Nancy made it so. We just called her Nancy. I'm not sure she'd like being called Auntie. Because she was cool, like our friend, but also strict and in charge when needed; she could walk that tightrope of friendly/discipline/caring that the best Academic Aunties do, whether working with teenagers, young adults, or Elders. You see, in community college in California, especially in those days when tuition was $11 a credit, there would be all kinds of students in class, including me, and we had some fabulous instructors, including Nancy who taught us in health and physical education classes.

Nancy was also our coach, our fearless leader, our motivator, as we ran mile after mile in cross-country and track. Drills. Stretching. Hill repeats. Weightlifting. Tempo runs. Speedwork. Fartlek (look it up if you don't know it).

Heart rate training. Cross-training. We learned so much from her! Nancy always had an encouraging word, no matter our skill level or 400-meter or mile split. I marvel at her ability to be completely invested in our success, runners who were two to three times slower than her—as she was a world-class professional athlete, sponsored to travel and race all around the globe. Despite her busy schedule, she never failed to show up for us, and her strong arms never tired of holding a believing mirror up to reflect back to us the great hope, potential, and belief that she saw in us, sending a clear message that we could dare to trust and believe in—we could finish a workout, or strive to do our personal best in a competition, or try a new track-and-field event we previously thought of as impossible.

When all the work of the day's practice was over, and if it was someone's birthday, we'd gather in Nancy's office, and there would be some kind of birthday treat: a cupcake, muffin, or brownie. If needed, a PowerBar would do. A candle would be lit. The ceremonial birthday crown would be set atop the honoree's head. We'd sing and clap, and Nancy would take photos to document it all. And then, after the sharing of treats was concluded, the birthday honoree got to do something fabulous. They would get to choose a gift from the prize box. Nancy's prize box consisted of different athletic goods, some new, some used. I think of it as the runner's equivalent to the dentist's office treasure chest. One time I chose a gently used pink sports bra. Now, some of you may think it's a little gross to be excited about a used sports bra, a hard-working garment that soaks up sweat. But let me tell you, as a college student paying rent in California, such a gift was much appreciated. Those garments are expensive!

At the end of each season, Nancy would gift each student athlete an envelope of photos from our time together. As we *oooooohed!* and *aaaaahed!* through our respective stack of photos, we'd always come across someone's birthday party in Nancy's office. I see the photo in my mind's eye: a bunch of sweaty people of many different ages, with backgrounds just as numerous, often someone had brought their children to practice (you get extra great training by pushing a stroller on those steep hill repeats!); a cupcake with a lit candle; the honoree wearing what some would call a tacky crown. And somewhere in the frame was the prize box, an empty copy paper box with assorted treasures.

It's a simple celebration, yet each honoree felt special, secure in the knowledge that there was a strong role model and a kind group of people who cared about us and who were happy to celebrate our presence. Each birthday honoree who wore the paper birthday crown knew they were special, that they mattered. Of course, the crown, gift, and treat were merely small symbols. The true gifts were that these experiences filled our hearts and inspired us to be better people. That's what a role model's kindness and care can do for us. I think that's the greatest lesson Nancy taught us.

Discussion/Journaling Questions for "Prize Box"

1. Think of a strong role model you've witnessed or known. What is one lesson they taught that you continue to treasure or value?

2. Has there been a time when you were given a gift you really appreciated? What was it? Or maybe you can think of a time when you gave a fabulous gift to someone else?

Birthday Month

In my family, birthdays are always celebrated. Some might say too much. But I would disagree.

Let me explain.

We do all of the, as far as I can tell, somewhat normal things. How does one really grasp what is normal when it's all we've ever known? It reminds me of when I was 17 years old and went away to the city, and my well-meaning and sincere classmates, dorm friends, and professors would ask things like, "What's it like to grow up on a reservation?" When I first encountered questions like this I would freeze. What do they mean? I'd wonder. It's normal, I'd think, but sensed that wasn't quite the right answer.

Then, I began to put the pieces together. My early training as a social scientist, someone who studies topics related to people and our society, began to unfold. I looked around my immediate surroundings and pointed out differences.

"We don't have tall buildings," I'd comment, dipping my toe into the water of explaining vast differences from the perspective of a teenager to largely other teenagers. (Later in college I would learn to name such differences in academic terms of social, economic, political, and racial analyses.) We'd ride the elevator up to our dorm floor, each toting a pint of Ben and Jerry's ice cream in our hands. "We don't have any elevators. There's no Ben and Jerry's ice cream," I'd offer, knowing my descriptions were inadequate but still feeling that mild frustration of a determined but not completely content Rubik's Cube solver who's not quite there yet. Not even by a long shot.

"Do you have shopping malls?" my new city friend might ask.

"No, not on the reservation. But in the cities off the reservation we do."

"Like where?" they'd ask, digging into their rich and sweet trendy ice cream.

"In Yakima."

"Wait. Isn't that your Tribe?"

"Yes. The city is named after us, but it isn't on the reservation. It's north of our reservation border."

Their smooth brows would furrow in contemplation and confusion. "Well, why isn't it on your reservation if it's named after your people?"

"The white people who first settled in the area, and the government, took it."

"Oh. That's messed up."

"Yeah. But our Tribe is strong, and we're always fighting for our land and our rights."

"Oh, that's good. Do you want to go to the library?"

And so conversations like this happened then, as they do now. Everyday questions, ideas, and exchanges about people, place, history, Tribal sovereignty. These are big topics that can be challenging to completely address. However, the pint-sized pieces of learning and sharing are good; while not perfect, they can be the beginning of shared understanding.

What I perhaps most learned through such exchanges is that it can take some work to figure out what is normal, or even to explain to an outsider what normal is. Because normal just "is."

I'm sharing all of this because it can be tricky to tell what normal birthday celebrating is within a family.

In my family, we do what I suspect may be "normal" things, like delivering or sending cards and gifts to each person each year, on or around their birthday, no matter what. It doesn't matter if they're sick or traveling, or moved far away for a job, or school, or a relationship you know is doomed but they have their silly "love goggles" on and can't see it yet.

They get the card and gift. Period. It's custom. It shows you remember them and lets them know they're special to you.

Now, if a social gathering (also known as a birthday party) can be arranged, with work, school, and kids' sports practices, etc. taken into account—if it is even 1% possible that a party can happen—it will. A parent or grandparent or sibling or aunt/uncle will step up and host it. Which also means they'll have a whole bunch of food and beverages to purchase and a bunch of dishes to wash. So it's a labor of love.

Now, we all probably understand the importance of someone's "special day" (a.k.a. their real birthday).

But in my family, we take it up a notch. We have the "birthday month."

Yes. This means all month long the birthday "monthee" gets special treatment, consideration, latitude on things like getting extra treats, help with chores, or being allowed to horn in on other people's plans.

"What? You're going out to eat? Well, I want to come! It's my birthday month!"

I've even seen it stretched so far as to take advantage of the day before one's birthday month begins.

"What? You're going to [insert fun outing or getting a tasty treat here]? What about me? It's my birthday month eve!"

And so it goes.

Ok, that last one, I think maybe I'm the only person who's used that one so far.

But you see what I mean. My family is one that nurtures that love, care, and zest for celebration that seems above and beyond. It might be tempting to see our zeal for birthdays as perhaps decadent or unnecessary. However, as I look through the lens of my Yakama cultural teachings, as well as my social science training, I see that a major reason our community is so strong and enduring is our fierce and kind dedication to the collective. We want what's best for one another, and we also trust, love, and respect that each person knows what's best for themselves. I'm so grateful. Now, whose birthday month is next?

Aunty + Uncle
P.O. Box 100
Yakama Rez
Happy Birthday!

Discussion/Journaling Questions for "Birthday Month"

1. Have you ever celebrated a special occasion for more than one day? Why or why not?

2. What is a custom that you treasure? Does everyone you know share the same custom? Describe some of the similarities and differences.

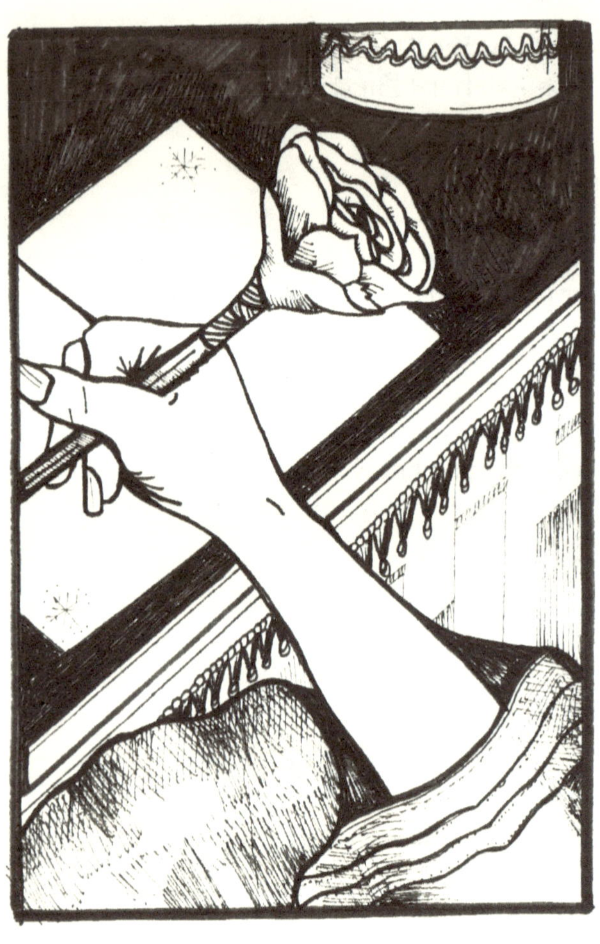

A Precious Birthday Celebration

Birthday celebrations are always, in some way, fun or precious. At least that's my experience. But they're sometimes fun in different ways.

Sometimes there's a festive pizza party for a child's birthday, with kids plunking quarters into arcade machines. If joined by grandparents or aunts or uncles, we are treated to an intergenerational battle for high score on pinball, Pac-Man, or Frogger. Or perhaps the group clusters around the grabby claw machine, as the player tries to time the exact placement and movement of the claw to grab and win a teddy bear, or digital watch, or some kind of fancy gold coin in a box.

Ahhhhhh! Near miss! Can I try again?

The kids, whether five or seventy-five years old, all have big smiles and their faces shine with joy, more beautifully shiny than the round disks of pepperoni atop the pizza.

Before attending the pizza party, guests

likely stopped by Toys "R" Us or Clover Leaf or Target, or maybe just the bank, to pick up a gift for the birthday honoree.

But other birthday celebrations have an entirely different flavor.

Sometimes the gift giver is searching for the gift in a little boutique store. It's tastefully decorated, the hard work of women who've put time and effort into making the store feel as much like a sanctuary as is possible. There's light, happy music playing in the background, the kind you might hear on the 40s Junction channel on SiriusXM.

The store has a gorgeous display of greeting cards. Some are handcrafted masterpieces. Some are the bearers of jokes that make you laugh out loud. Some have humor specific to the place. You see the one your friend sent to your loved one earlier this month. "Chemo sucks," the cover says in bold writing. Inside the card, "I hope it sucks the cancer right out of you!" You smile and chuckle softly. Our people have deep expertise in finding the humor among the tragedy. Yet we also carry the frustration of wondering, *How many times will we be asked to do this?* You take a deep breath and place the card back in its spot on the rack.

You choose a card with a summer mountain scene, a beautiful blue sky and majestic evergreen trees. You notice part of the proceeds go to cancer research, and you say a silent message of gratitude for the people working so hard to find better treatments and a cure. Card decided, you move over to the rack displaying pretty hats of every color, size, and texture. They're all so different! But you notice inside they are all the same—soft material that will cradle, comfort, and warm your loved one's head; their tender scalp has lost so much hair.

Choosing the hat, you're a bit choked up, fighting tears, although you see the Kleenex box nearby and realize your response is not unique. You choose a pretty blue hat with a short brim. Practical but with a unique style, just like your loved one who's connected to the machines upstairs. Gift and card in hand, you go to the register. The attendant smiles gently, offers to remove the price tag and wrap your gift for you.

"Yes, please," you respond.

"Would you like a pen to fill out the card?" the thoughtful attendant offers.

You nod.

She hands you a pen with a huge artificial rose taped to the top.

You smile at the large yellow flower. It's just like the ones on the rosebush back home you planted with your loved one.

You complete the card and put it in its

envelope. You notice the attendant has timed their gift wrapping to end just when you are done.

"How about some candies?" She offers you a bowl of individually wrapped hard candies.

"Yes, thank you," and you grab a few for the long car ride home, knowing your loved one's mouth and throat may have sores the candy can help soothe.

These women at the cancer center gift shop, they think of everything; they are angels. It feels good to have someone else do the thinking, worrying, planning, caring. You smile at the attendant, grab a couple Kleenexes for your pocket, and head back to the elevator.

Inside the elevator in a rare moment of privacy, you cry. You're angry, upset, sad, annoyed, confused.

Why this disease? Why your loved one?

You use the gift shop Kleenex to mop up your face, tears, and snot, saturating them. You compose yourself as the elevator dings and opens to the familiar floor. You throw the used Kleenex away and take a generous squirt of hand sanitizer. You feel better now, having let those tears out, kind of like the Instant Pot when it's done cooking and you turn the little lever on top, "psssssssss!" the steam shoots out, pressure released. You laugh a little, thinking of yourself as an Instant Pot. It's a cool appliance. Mostly, you're happy to be in a better mood, a mood befitting a birthday celebration.

You walk into your loved one's curtained cubicle, "Happy birthday!" you say loudly, hoping to gather a crowd to help you sing. It works. Soon several of the staff help you sing the "Happy Birthday" song, and everyone claps and smiles at the end. You present your gift to your loved one. Of course, you nailed it. They feel so special receiving your perfect card and gift.

As they sit in the hospital bed receiving their treatment, they pat you on the hand and thank you.

"Every birthday is a gift," they tell you. "Another year of life. How special. How lucky I am," they share their hard-earned wisdom with you.

You smile and nod in agreement.

It's not a festive pizza party, with Pac-Man and grabby claw games, but you're together. Your hearts and minds are full of love and care. It's a precious birthday celebration.

ALING .

Discussion/Journaling Questions for "A Precious Birthday Celebration"

1. In this story, the narrator shares the gratitude and relief they feel when a stranger is kind and thoughtful. Have you ever experienced the kindness of strangers? Think of a way perhaps you could be the kind and thoughtful person blessing the day of someone you don't know.

2. The narrator describes hard-earned wisdom being shared at the end of the story. Who in your life has shared wisdom with you? What is a wise message you might like to share?

Non-Birthday Party

Sometimes people say they don't like their birthdays. In such a case, if a family member or friend says with excitement, "It's your birthday next week!" they may be met with a grumpy, "What are you so excited about? Mind your own business."

Hmmmmm…this can be a delicate situation. And for birthday fans like myself, it can feel like a direct challenge, a puzzle I must help solve.

Now, this whole situation might sound problematic to you. And you're probably right. It's a tangled business. If you've ever gone a week without combing your hair and the day of reckoning comes and you can feel that mound of tangled hair that must be eased out with a brush, comb, or pick, you know what I mean.

So for us birthday enthusiasts, when we come across a loved one who's anti-birthday, we want to get in there with our sparkly celebrating comb and help untangle that. We can't help ourselves! We actually have a whole tool belt full of combs, picks, and brushes we can try, switching tactics as needed. We may start with something like, "I'm going to have a family dinner at my house on Saturday night."

"What the hell for? That's my birthday, and I don't want a dinner. I hate the fuss and the cake and singing and candles. I don't want a dinner."

Go to the tool belt. Choose another comb.

"Well, it's not a birthday dinner for you. Mom just asked me to have everyone over."

See, the strategy is to pin the blame on an older, more authoritative family member…

"Yeah, right. You just want to have a party because you like parties. You like cake. I don't. I don't want my birthday celebrated."

Hmmmmm…this is a tough tangle. Another comb swap. Let's try a pick this time.

"I told you. It's not a birthday party. It's a family dinner. If you want, we can all wear T-shirts that say "This is not a birthday party." And we're not having cake. Mom asked Sis-in-Law to bake two of her huckleberry pies and to bring real whipped cream. But you don't have to come if you don't want to. You can be rude to Mom and Sis-in-Law if you want. I have no problem eating your piece of huckleberry pie."

Their face softens. Of course they'll attend if the most delicious dessert in the world is on the menu.

You fight a smile, as you can tell the non-birthday-party birthday party will be a success.

Now for the clincher, at the stealthy birthday party have one of the cute, sweet kids in your family quietly go up to the birthday grinch and present them with a homemade card and tell them "Happy birthday" and "I love you." Then, after the hugs and kisses are over, serve the pie. Then have all the kids bring in the birthday gifts that were stockpiled in the other room, or under a blanket in the corner.

There may not be any singing, candles, or brightly colored decorations. But there will be a gathering of loved ones who get to sit together to say with a gift, card, or simply their presence:

I love you.

I am so glad you're alive and with us another year.

You matter to me.

That's one of the things I love most about birthdays. They seem like they're only about the birthday honoree. But really they're about the love, kindness, and thoughtfulness of a collective. Sometimes humble, shy people we care about kind of dread the attention lavished on them. Isn't that a lovely paradox—that sometimes the people most deserving of honors and gifts do their best to avoid receiving them? Sometimes we find ways of honoring them despite their protests. And when the gift giving is done, sure, the honoree has a nice pile of goodies to take home, and in fact all attendees take with them perhaps the greatest gift of all: affirmation of the love, joy, and connection among every person in our collective.

At the end of the non-party party, you hug your loved one and they touch your smooth tangle-free hair and you do likewise. Without words, you both say, "Thank you" and "I love you." It's another birthday successfully non-celebrated with just the perfect celebration.

Discussion/Journaling Questions for "Non-Birthday Party"

1. Have you or someone you know been reluctant to receive attention or gifts? How did you resolve the situation? What did you learn from the experience?

2. Think of a time when something seemed to be about an individual but was actually about a community coming together to share something important or fun. What do you think about these occasions?

$500

At the Shopping Mall

I love the hype surrounding birthdays and holidays. Perhaps the greatest hype of all happens around Christmas. All the planning of food, parties, travel, decorations, choosing a tree, cards, lights, gift wrap, and oh so much more!

I remember one Christmas season I saw a family Christmas sweater set display in the store at the mall. The purpose of which was so the family wardrobe coordinator—likely one of the moms, I assume—could walk up to that one display in the store and get matching or complementary (for those afraid to be too matchy-matchy) sweaters for the entire family. One-stop shopping for the tops needed for an annual Christmas card photoshoot. Brilliant! I love it! I smiled big, thinking of various families filing out of minivans at a carefully selected location, lighting at just the right time of day. Kids' hair neatly combed and sprayed, we will get that cowlick down. I hope the family dog got a matching sweater or bow too! Dogs love that, you know. Then after the most perfect photo is captured, send it in to Costco or

Shutterfly, etc., and soon it will grace the fridge or mantle of all the loved ones of the sweater-matching family.

I love it! What joy this sweater display has given me. I continue my stroll through the mall.

I smell air freshener that smells like gingersnap cookies. Mmmmm...I love those cookies, all shiny with a sugar crust from the baker rolling the doughball in sugar just before baking. I always underbake them, so they're soft, as I prefer my cookies. Although I know tea drinkers sometimes like a crispy cookie to dunk in their tea. Oh well. To each their own.

I continue my walk through the mall. Now I'm in the atrium, and Santa is sitting in a huge chair under a gazebo. Children and their adults are lined up. I hope they all get exactly what they wish for, and more. I think it's a nice tradition, this Santa at the mall thing, but I do admit part of me gets nervous anytime a child sits in a stranger's lap. Well, it's Christmas! Let's not dwell on that thought too long.

Now, if you live in an area where Christian churches have influence and political power, there may even be a nativity display at the mall, at which you'll see the star of Bethlehem, a manger, likely at least one angel, Joseph, Mary, Jesus, a few barnyard animals, and perhaps the three wise men. I look closer at the manger scene. Mary's looking pretty good for just having had her first child, all natural birth, in a pile of straw. Holy Mother indeed! Joseph looks like he's playing it cool. What faith. What strength. And, of course, in the middle of it all is the birthday boy, Jesus. He's got the biggest hoopla around his birthday of anyone I know. And as I've told you earlier in this book, I know a lot of good birthday celebrators.

Now, some people don't like the commercial hype around Christmas. I think that's the message behind the bumper stickers I sometimes see, "Jesus Is the Reason for the Season."

People from diverse faith and spiritual backgrounds may sometimes feel their celebrations and traditions are overlooked and overshadowed by the Christmas hype: Diwali, Hanukkah, Kwanzaa, Winter Solstice. These are beautiful and special times of celebration.

Yet looking again at the manger scene, we all suspect Jesus' birthday will continue to dominate. Who knew the story of a poverty-stricken girl in what we now call the Middle East giving birth in a pile of straw in a barn would be such a big deal? The manger scene is so iconic, urging us to think of the sacred in a profane setting. I look again at the figurine of Mary. I say a silent prayer that all young women and their bodies will be understood as sacred in our society—just like the mural at our Tribe's Yakamart gas station in Toppenish says, "No More Stolen Sisters." How hard my community is praying that this basic human right will soon be upheld, a world without gender-based violence, a world in which all girls, women, and two-spirit relatives are safe and respected.

My thoughts returning back to the mall, I notice the nativity scene here is kind of white-washed, with all but one of the wise men's skin tones looking rather pale. Speaking of pale, it is my view that this nativity scene pales in comparison to many that I have seen prominently displayed on my reservation, including in some homes, which have remade the famous scene in a Native American theme—instead of a manger, the birthplace is a ts'xwiilí (teepee). Human figurines are clothed in buckskin garments, and their dark hair is graced with an eagle feather or two, or perhaps feathers are attached to a headband or headdress. Coyote, bison, eagle, deer, or elk may be part of the sacred setting. When I gaze upon such a display, I can't help but think Jesus would've been a great Pow Wow dancer. I wonder in what dance style he would have specialized. Fancy, probably, I think to myself. Gosh, I wonder which Auntie would have made his regalia? Holy moly. I bet that would be something to see.

Google shows it's almost 7,000 miles from Bethlehem to Wapato. The Holy Family definitely would get the prize for traveling the farthest distance to attend our Pow Wow. "Sorry, good people from Arizona, you didn't travel the farthest this year," our MC would have to tell the disappointed folx from the southwest.

Oh! My attention is drawn back to my surroundings at the shopping mall, as I see some kids are getting ready to play Christmas songs on the piano atop a small nearby stage. I love piano recitals. I better go get a good seat. I love the effort the children place in the songs they've worked hard to learn for this moment, this day, their holiday recital. Whether they are beginners just learning the keys and how to read music or seasoned experts who dazzle us with complex pieces memorized and played with perfection, I clap fiercely for each musician. I know how hard it can be to get up on that stage. Their effort is a blessing to us.

After the recital, beautiful music still fresh in my memory, I go home and make gingersnaps, underbaked, soft and chewy. Mmmmm…

I open the mail, and I see a beautiful family with matching sweaters wishing me the greetings of the season. My face crinkles with a delighted smile as I reach for a magnet to proudly display my loved ones on the fridge.

Whatever particular festivities bring a smile to your face, I hope you are showered with all that warms your heart and lifts your spirit, every season of the year.

Discussion/Journaling Questions for "At the Shopping Mall"

1. In this story, the narrator describes the joy of receiving a special card in the mail. Have you experienced such joy? If so, perhaps you can thank the person who sent you the card. Maybe you can share joy by sending a card to one of your loved ones.

2. In "At the Shopping Mall," the narrator reflects on the sacred in a profane (or everyday) setting. When have you experienced something sacred or extraordinary in everyday life? How did you know you were witnessing something important or rich with meaning?

Note: You can read more about the "No More Stolen Sisters" mural at https://www.smokesignals.org/articles/2020/02/27/tribal-member-creates-murals-to-honor-murdered-missing-indigenous-women/

Happy Birthday, Grandpa

Sometimes birthdays are times of excitement, joy, and happy anticipation. Sometimes, however, birthdays can bring up feelings that don't feel like celebrating. At times like these, it helps me to remember that my feelings around birthdays can be complex. I believe all feelings are important, as each feeling invites us to understand something about the world around us and within us. We're invited to understand in a new, deeper, richer way. When I pause to remember this, I see and trust my feelings as the treasured teachers I know they can be.

For example, today is my grandpa's birthday. And I feel a sense of sadness, loss, and grief today. This surprises me as I am a generally happy person looking for reasons to celebrate. But instead of those easy, light feelings, today I have a combination of feelings that leaves me with a sense of heaviness, doubt, uncertainty, brokenness, and an overall blah. Thinking is harder. Doing is harder. Slower.

I feel equally torn. Half of me wants to rush into my day full of work tasks and busyness, with a faint hope that doing more, more, more will throw open the shutters of my feelings to air them out and usher in a new set of feelings—more comfortable and fun ones perhaps.

And the other half of me says in a deep, wise voice I think of as being close to spirit, "No, don't rush, don't move at a pace intended to be faster, doing more. Have the courage to sit with these feelings, to companion them—to accept, understand, and comfort yourself—just as your most treasured loved ones have modeled for you again and again. Trust that you are enough. You do enough. You have all you need to heal and be whole, to see you are already whole."

Pausing to listen to that inner wisdom helps. I smile in recognition of the truth: I am whole. Grateful to be grasping this lesson, which allows me to make room for treasured memories of a person who showed me love and care. Tears come to my eyes as I envision my grandpa as I knew him, an elderly man sitting in the big wooden chair at my parents' kitchen table, his chocolatey brown eyes shining with kindness, and perhaps a bit of mischievousness.

My grandpa died when I was young. There's no logical reason for me to carry a sense of loss and grief today, the anniversary of the day when he was born. Except I also know that tomorrow is the anniversary of his death. We've seen that more than once—when an Elder lives just long enough to celebrate one more birthday. When I was young I wondered about that—did they do that because they enjoyed the cake? Songs? Gifts? Seeing the whole family gather for a fun celebration? I don't know. Maybe I won't until my time comes to leave this world. Maybe I'll never know. And that's okay. Just as all my feelings are okay. Just as any feelings stirred up by birthdays are okay.

Happy birthday, Grandpa.

I imagine when I next look in the mirror I'll see a sight that honors him and his legacy: chocolatey brown eyes shining with kindness, and perhaps a bit of mischievousness.

Discussion/Journaling Questions for "Happy Birthday, Grandpa"

1. In this story, the narrator describes the importance of trusting feelings as "treasured teachers." Think of a time when you trusted and learned from your feelings. What lesson did you learn? Or maybe you can remember a time you were able to mostly or fully accept how you were feeling. Describe the situation and how it felt to have self-acceptance.

2. Do you ever feel the need to engage in busyness to cope with complex feelings? Or are you more likely to pause and "companion" complex feelings? The next time complex feelings arise, how might you like to approach them? What message do you most want to tell yourself when you are perhaps struggling?

ḳápashaayat

Birthdays beyond the Binary

In my experience, children typically enjoy birthday celebrations. They're fun, lighthearted, and exciting.

But they can also be cruel. Exclusionary. In grade school there can be cool kid parties and less-than-cool kid parties. A singsongy "You're not invited" might be rubbed in someone's face during recess. Children can be cruel; it's learned behavior. It can be unlearned, thankfully.

Some faith traditions and families don't celebrate birthdays. A well-meaning parent or Auntie who brings cake or cupcakes for the entire classroom might overlook this. What patience the child abstaining from celebrating has while everyone sings and claps and eats the sugary, colorful treat.

And what about our gluten-free friends? Or those who are choosing a vegan lifestyle? Well, that can be a tough situation. Wheat flour and dairy tend to reign supreme in birthday treats. But we are wising up. We can bring a bag of tangerines, for example, to provide dietary choice options for people with food allergies, animal product–free diets, diabetes, or who simply have learned the lesson of avoiding sugary treats.

In this book, I've written about ways that birthday celebrations can and do bring us together. They can make us feel special, cared for, like who we are matters. I'll tell you, I love a princess party for a little girl, or a Tonka truck party for a little boy! Yet we've probably all seen or experienced how birthdays can divide us, alienate us, even from ourselves.

I'm thinking now about the young person known by others as a little boy who wants nothing more than a doll to play with for his or their birthday, but he or they are shamed and hushed, perhaps even slapped across the face for saying so.

I'm thinking of the young person known by others as a little girl who wants wrestling gear or a football and can't wait to try out for these sports when she or they finally reaches seventh grade in school. By the way, she or they plans to work construction for a living if she or they doesn't make it into the NFL. Her or their family and classmates may roll their eyes or laugh at the young person, or worse.

These children and their birthday wishes are precious. They are not the status quo, fitting neatly into society's tidy little gender binary with narrow views of "girls should be like this" and "boys should be like that." These binary, rigid either/or limited views of human possibility can be painful, and they can needlessly limit the brilliance and achievement of so many.

Look around! Look outside! Do you see it? The beautiful wisdom and gifts of Creation? Do you see Aan (Sun) rising every morning to warm our planet? We depend on Sun, who is both a holy being and an everyday companion. And guess what? Sun is a gender bender! In some of our Yakama traditional stories, Sun is a male figure, strong and handsome. In other stories, Sun is female, warm, nurturing, and generous.

Sun is all of these things and more. I love it! Wisdom from the Sky.

Let's embrace the beautiful lesson and cherish all children and their brilliant and unique contributions, whether they fit inside our expectations or blast them apart, inviting us to think differently. When we do this, we can see the world in a whole new way. We can see shining new possibilities for the young person and ourselves.

I'm so happy it's time to celebrate birthdays beyond the binary. Would you like a cupcake or tangerine? Or both? Why not?!

Discussion/Journaling Questions for "Birthdays beyond the Binary"

1. Have you ever felt excluded or left out in some way? How did that experience help you be more thoughtful in how you treat other people?

2. In this story, the narrator hopes that all children can be affirmed for their brilliance and uniqueness. In what ways do you celebrate your own brilliance and uniqueness? Who is someone you admire who has disrupted the status quo or expected way of being?

Note: If you like Yakama stories, you will enjoy the book *Anakú Iwachá: Yakama Legends and Stories.* Learn more about the book at https://uwapress.uw.edu/book/9780295748245/anaku-iwacha/

If you would like to learn about gender pronouns, this web page from my alma mater's Gender Equity Center is a helpful resource: https://www.csusm.edu/gec/pronounsmatter.html

Conclusion: A Special Invitation

As we near the end of this book, I would like to invite you back to a special birthday celebration. My sweet dog, Anahúy, was born in October, a lovely month when, in our northern climate, we witness cooler days and nights, and it's such a relief from the hot summers. This is a beautiful time of change in fall colors—leaves dazzling us with their showy displays. It is also the time when the length of days becomes shorter and when sweet apples are harvested across my beloved Yakama homeland. The hard work of the harvest is done by peoples from many Indigenous communities. What great effort it takes; shoulders, backs, and legs strong from the non-stop effort of reaching, picking apples, and placing the famous fruit into bins to be trucked to warehouses in Wapato and Yakima, where they are packed into boxes and sent to markets all around the world.

Like many dogs, one of Anahúy's greatest joys is to go for a walk. When I take a break from work, or maybe on the weekend, I'll sometimes remember to make time for this special occasion. I'll look at him and ask in an enthusiastic voice, "Do you want to go for a walk?!" The answer is always a resounding Ii! (Yes!) with a wagging of his tail so boisterous his whole body moves.

He jumps with excitement, not the high jumps of his youth with forepaws pushing on my torso and nearly knocking me down. Rather, now he jumps just a bit, a few inches off the ground, in a kind of graceful and delicate way, a motion befitting his snout that is now a bit distinguished with white hair marking his status as a mature dog.

When we walk in the apple orchard by my parents' house, Anahúy is greeted by a fabulous birthday treat buffet—sweet apples that have fallen on the ground. He adores apples and finds delight in this fruit on the ground that will not go to market.

Sometimes we'll take a special trip to the mountains for Anahúy's birthday. He's great at finding birthday treats wherever he goes. Maybe he'll lap up water from a tiny pond made in a dirt road's pothole—filled with last night's rain from plump-looking clouds that came in with the breeze from the Pacific Ocean. Or maybe Anahúy will trot through mud and then savor cleaning his paws later. Or maybe he'll enjoy simply sniffing the pristine forest air; he relishes delightful scents, which I can't detect, brought by the slightest of breezes.

On our walks, when I remember to pay attention, I'm amazed at what a fabulous teacher my dog is. He reminds me of the important lessons I'm still trying to learn:

Savor the present moment.

Find delight in the gifts all around me.

Understand and celebrate what brings me joy.

I smile with gratitude at my teacher, a humble shelter dog no one else wanted, and I can't believe how full my heart feels in receiving these gifts on a walk to celebrate his birthday.

Isn't that how the best gift giving goes? You put thought and care into giving something to a loved one—only to find that the gratitude and kindness you thought you were giving away actually return even bigger to you. I think this is the process in which seeds of wisdom are planted and nurtured within us. We learn to cultivate them as we age, soaking up the beautiful lessons all around us. This might be how Elders become so wise.

As we conclude our birthday walk in the mountains, Hulí (Wind) returns, and beautiful, golden-colored Niní (Aspen Tree) leaves dance and fall gracefully through the air before resting on the forest floor. I do believe Mother Nature is throwing her confetti to celebrate

Anahúy's birthday. What a gift. And a perfect conclusion to our birthday celebration.

Thank you for joining us.

About the Illustrator

Crystal L. Buck is a Native American artist and resides in Spokane, Washington. She is an enrolled member of the Yakama Nation and grew up on the Yakama Indian Reservation. Her passion for drawing and painting evolved at a very young age. She gives credit to her amazing art teachers. They encouraged her and believed in her talent enough to enter her work in local shows throughout the years. Before completing high school, she participated in her first painting showcase where she met and networked with various artists. She sold her first piece in 1997. Upon graduating from college as an Exercise Specialist in 2003, she also received a minor in art with a specialization in painting from Fort Lewis College in Durango, Colorado. Most recently, she collaborated with the Burke Museum in Seattle, Washington, to create signage for their re-opening after COVID-19. Her drawing was selected for the 2019–2020 Washington State Indian Education Program logo. In 2020, Crystal illustrated the books *The Auntie Way: Stories Celebrating Kindness, Fierceness, and Creativity; Huckleberries & Coyotes: Lessons from Our More than Human Relations*; and in 2021,

Fox Doesn't Wear a Watch: Lessons from Mother Nature's Classroom.

Crystal is the mother of four beautiful children and loves spending time with her family. She enjoys participating in traditional gatherings and learning the Salish language with her kids. She's passionate about running, leading fitness dance classes, drawing, and crafting. She is inspired by artistic creations that focus on her Native roots, modern art techniques, Zentangle, vibrant and various uses of colors, lines, and patterns. One of her artistic dreams is to blend her love for hummingbirds and her individual style into a unique thematic masterpiece. You may contact Crystal by email: cry5tal_lea@yahoo.com

About the Author

Dr. Michelle M. Jacob is an enrolled member of the Yakama Nation and has over 20 years of teaching experience, most currently at the University of Oregon where she is Professor of Indigenous Studies in the Department of Education Studies and serves as Affiliated Faculty in the Department of Indigenous, Race, and Ethnic Studies and Affiliated Faculty in the Environmental Studies Program. Michelle engages in scholarly and activist work that seeks to understand and work toward a holistic sense of health and well-being within Indigenous communities and among allies who wish to engage decolonization.

Michelle loves to write and has published eight books, including *Huckleberries & Coyotes, The Auntie Way*, and *Yakama Rising*. She has also published numerous articles in social science, education, and health science research journals and has been awarded grants from the U.S. Department of Education, the National Endowment for the Humanities, Spencer Foundation, and the National Science Foundation. Her research areas of interest include Indigenous methodologies, spirituality, health, education, Native feminisms, and decolonization.

Michelle founded Anahuy Mentoring, LLC to support her vision of sharing Indigenous methodologies with a broad audience. Michelle is grateful to all her family and friends for their love and support and, of course, keeps learning and re-learning lessons as she sweetly savors each year of her fabulous life.

Michelle absolutely adores working with writers. Maybe you want to join all the fabulous writers in the Auntie Way Writing Retreat? Learn more and register for the next session at https://anahuy-mentoring.mn.co/

You may contact Michelle through the form on her website, where you can also sign up for her email list to receive all the news related to Anahuy Mentoring:
https://anahuymentoring.com

Follow Michelle on Twitter:
@AnahuyMentoring

Author Acknowledgments

I am grateful to the fantastic scholars and educators who reviewed this book manuscript: Marta Clifford, Django Paris, Amy Lonetree, and Meggin McIntosh. Chris Andersen and Theresa Jacob also offered valuable feedback on the manuscript. Thanks to Alja Kooistra for skillful copyediting. All feedback I received greatly strengthened this manuscript, and any weaknesses remain my own. I am grateful *Birthday Gifts: Honoring People and Places We Love* is blessed with the beautiful artwork of Crystal Buck. Many thanks to all of the wonderful writers in the Auntie Way Writing Retreat as well as readers of my blog and Anahuy Mentoring email subscribers; your kind encouragement of my work keeps me inspired!

Much gratitude to my dear colleagues at the University of Oregon: Sapsik'ʷałá (Teacher) Education Program, Education Studies, Native American and Indigenous Studies, Native Strategies, and the COE Finance team.

Huge baskets full of thanks to my family: Dad, Mom, Uncle Jim, Roger, Gina, Garret, Hunter, Faith, Justin, Alicia, Quintic, Hazen, Blaise, Sealy, and my in-laws, who are a blessing!

I'll end by thanking the world's greatest camping and hiking buddies, Chris and Anahúy. I love our blessed time together as we continue to be nurtured and inspired by the beauty of N'chi-Wána and her tributaries. Áwna!

About Anahuy Mentoring

Anahuy Mentoring is committed to engaging Indigenous methodologies to teach about the importance of Indigenous ways of knowing and being. *Birthday Gifts: Honoring People and Places We Love* is published by Anahuy Mentoring, an independent Indigenous press that utilizes Indigenous cultural values in peer review.

Learn more and join my email list at https://anahuymentoring.com

Follow on Twitter: @AnahuyMentoring

Anahúy is the Yakama Ichishkíin word for black bear.

Made in United States
Troutdale, OR
10/30/2023